THE IRRELEVANT MAN

ESSENTIAL POETS SERIES 226

Guernica Editions Inc. acknowledges the support of
the Canada Council for the Arts and the Ontario Arts Council.
The Ontario Arts Council is an agency of the Government of Ontario.
We acknowledge the financial support of the Government of Canada through
the National Translation Program for Book Publishing for our translation
activities. We also acknowledge the financial support of the Government of
Canada through the Canada Book Fund (CBF) for our publishing activities.

ANTONIO D'ALFONSO

THE
IRRELEVANT
·MAN

GUERNICA
TORONTO – BUFFALO – LANCASTER (U.K.)
2014

Michael Mirolla, Editor
Guernica Editions Inc.
P.O. Box 76080, Abbey Market, Oakville (ON), Canada L6M 3H5
2250 Military Road, Tonawanda, N.Y. 14150-6000 U.S.A.

Typesetting and cover conception by Antonio D'Alfonso

Distributors:
University of Toronto Press Distribution,
5201 Dufferin Street, Toronto, (ON), Canada M3H 5T8
Gazelle Book Services, White Cross Mills, High Town, Lancaster LA1 4XS U.K.

First edition.
Printed in Canada.

Legal Deposit – First Quarter
National Library of Canada
Library of Congress Catalog Card Number: 2013953834
Library and Archives Canada Cataloguing in Publication
D'Alfonso, Antonio, 1953-, author
The irrelevant man / Antonio D'Alfonso.
(Essential poets series ; 226)
Poems.
Issued in print and electronic formats.
ISBN 978-1-55071-840-9 (pbk.).— ISBN 978-1-55071-841-6 (epub).—
ISBN 978-1-55071-842-3 (mobi)
I. Title. II. Series: Essential poets series ; 226
PS8557.A456I77 2014   C811'.54   C2013-907537-2
                                               C2013-907538-0

Contents

Dear Parents	11
And Me Among You	13
The Beginning	27
Two-Headed Man	32
The Futile Man	34
Zombies	36
Pier 21: Welcome	37
09.11.03	39
Where to Go	40
Back to Square One	43
26.07.02	45
The Stranger Stammers	46
05.11.05	47
Urbs aurea	49
Exile	53
To F., in memoriam	56
Daughter	58
A Father, a Daughter	59
09.04.02	61
The Devil Does Not Want	63
Your Body	65
30.05.12	66
The Nightmare	67
Night Drive	68
18.05.02	70
Uprooting	71
Intruder	76
Interlude	79
The Universe Is Calling	80
Paris Is Far	81
On Stage	82
Meschin	83
The Devil's Stiff Neck	85
The Forest	88
What Does This Politician Want?	89

Soldier   90
An Aside   91
Standing Behind Death   92
Prima donna   93
Slammer or Licker   94
Girl Friends   95
Like Setsuko Hara   96
Cleopatra and Anthony   97
Casanova   99
19.11.10   100
16.02.06   101
23.05.01   102
What a Wonderful Day   103
Whiteness   104
She Says   105
The Suns   106
Plagiarized Poem   107
Broccoli   108
Riddles   109
Insomnia   114
Taxi   115
Hollywood, Florida   116
Bob Dylan   117
At Last   119
Amazonia   120
Handsome Man   121
Italian Alphabet   125
Dante   126
Allora Gino   129

Notes   133

TO ELISA
MIA FIGLIA

I wanted to pursue the theme of the "weak" man who is no fighter in terms of his outward attributes but whom I none the less see as a victor of this life... weakness... the true price and hope of life. I have always liked people who can't adapt themselves to life pragmatically... people whose strength lies in their spiritual conviction and who take upon themselves a responsibility for others. Such people are often rather like children, only with the motivation of adults; from a common-sense point of view their position is unrealistic as well as selfless.

Andrei Tarkovsky

Dear Parents

Jugar, this is how, in 1190, Raimbaut de Vaquieras named the joker who tried to seduce married women. Back then people spoke a pluricultural language, a popular idiom (which I prefer to the word "vulgar"). *Volgo:* he who does not belong to the elite. In spite of your wish to see me belong to the elite of the continent, so well protected at that, I still consider myself a failure, an outsider. Unable to speak any dialect properly (not Guglionesano, not Tuscan, not English, not French), I am a writer without a voice. I have neither language, nor alphabet. You must forgive me for turning out to be an impostor of literature. I am a dumb joker of kings and queens. The few books I have read on the subject have taught me that *Itaglia* was a more unified country when it was divided. Had the master of the land sat himself more often at the table of his serfs, he would most certainly have helped write a history book with a happier ending. During one of the suppers, a new sort of passion would have risen and would have overturned, like tables, the social classes and religious differences. Conjectures. This morning I am honoured to be sitting at your breakfast table, tasting the music of your language that no poet has ever codified with the rules of the written word. You have no idea what sadness I feel knowing that the day you pass away, our language and history will die as well, for me and Elisa, your granddaughter, my daughter, who loves you so dearly. Which reader will I then seduce without our dialect?

Tonino

PS.

I had this text unrolling in me for a number of years. Many changes in the older me living with my ageing parents. Tough times. Have become obsessed by the future death of my parents, my relatives, my friends. By my life so mediocre. I have grown ignorant, I know less than I used to. An Italian translator reminded me how my parents were prohibited to speak their dialect by the Fascist regime. This text has been waiting to come out of me for sixty years. Had I been a poet living during World War II, I would have been arrested for speaking and writing in my dialect. To write out loud is a privilege given me for losing my maternal tongue. Sadness. Bacioni.

And Me Among You

'Tis very certain the desire of life
*   Prolongs it: this is obvious to physicians,*
When patients, neither plagued with friends nor wife,
*   Survive through very desperate conditions,*
Because they still can hope, nor shines the knife
*   Nor shears of Atropos before their visions,*
Despair of all recovery spoils longevity,
And makes men's miseries of alarming brevity.

Lord Byron

Do me a favor, cry.

John Cassavetes

1

May the Muses find me a home,
  I who have never had a home.
These goddesses have their darlings,
  Don't open their gates to strangers.
George B. Shaw proposes laughter
  When criticizing one's country.
The sponge I am is bleeding.
So many would like to see me hang.

2

I've walked into a Western film.
  Dressed to the hilt as a cowboy.
There, the desert; here, the city.
  No holster, no derringer.
My face unshaven, my hair uncut.
  The sun, high noon, too hot to bear.
No cloud in the sun-setting sky.
No truth deep in my pockets.

3

The mirage is on the horizon.
    Horse cantering is on the sound track.
Jean-Marc, as a Mohawk, smiles:
    What are you doing? he asks.
His fingers to his lips: *Food? Milk?*
    These metaphors are ridiculous.
Better to rhyme than to go crazy.
In all countries, prisons galore.

4

Territories are gloomy cages
    For the lonely beings we've become.
All horizons should be conquered,
    Every conquest abandonned.
A native is a well-bred tourist,
    Each smuggler a screaming teen.
Like Garibaldi in Uruguay,
We're scared of dying alone.

5

We should blossom, we should escape,
    We've got to leave our place to others.
The city sheriff does not want
    The weak to marry his sisters.
May those who don't assimilate
    Vacate our forefather's estate.
We might love, might hate, might have children.
No patch of land bestows a right.

6

Landowners are quick to ostracize.
    He for party, he for faith,
He for language, he for sect,
    He for being, he for non-being,
He from here, he from elsewhere.
    He is always afraid. But let's laugh
At our truths and mockeries.
Followers do not have farmers' hands.

7

Political art is an oxymoron.
    Trajectory bumps head with territory.
Don't want to go in circles,
    Then leave your gable, hop onto your van.
The soil beneath your feet yells for relay.
    Agriculture brought forth culture.
I know you laugh, my ideas
Go against what is shown on TV.

8

Philology is the study of
    Heroic texts, and finds its source
In Homeric verse. More than five hundred
    Years of patriotic alchemy
To fashion Europe the beautiful.
    The same potion was served to change
Giovanni Florio the Wop
Into William Shakespeare the Brit.

9

A nation spends quite a bit of cash
    To convert its citizens and
Turn them into soldiers.
    It procures pleasure, it boosts lofty airs
To see your brother in the limelight.
    You do not build a country
With your brother, but with your enemy.
How do you marry your opponent?

10

The stranger who rejects your god
    It is with him that you should deal.
No future without negotiation.
    The funnel widens at its rim,
Never at its narrow ring.
    We walk together, in parallel,
Criss-crossing, deviating, going on,
Learning from the Other, hand in hand.

11

Let's go back to the foreigner.

     My friend and I, side by side, there

Horses; in the distance, the tribes.

     Handful of dreams, spoonful of fears,

Pasta, wine, laughs, questions, pleadings.

     That Richard change to Riccardo

Or Dick don't change the stuff he's made of.

Is he or is he not the Master of the land?

12

Not a film by Lords on the Others.

     But films by Others on Others.

A gaze rising inside going

     Outside, a considerate gaze.

Of self, by self, against self.

     For others. Come from self as others.

Then imagine the opposite.

All of self as told by the Other.

13

Turtle Island has settled down
     On Earth. Our centre, a longhouse,
We, the Haudenosaunees,
     We are friends of Marx and Engels.
Ours is an unmatched constitution,
     Marvellous, yet quickly dwarfed.
From the sixteenth to the twentieth
Century, fifteen to thirty thousand souls gone.

14

We from Longhouse, we from Grande Île,
     We, ancient mothers from Six Nations,
I, Canasatego, I, Tadodaho,
     I, Dekanawidah, I, Joseph Brant,
We blare against how our gold,
     Our squash, our corn, our bean, our potato,
Helped finance our genocide,
Ordered by Louis XIV.

15

When you speak in our name,

    We tremble hiding in our cellars.

In sixteen hundred and sixty-four,

    The King assassinates in French.

In seventeen hundred and eighty-three,

    The King assassinates in English.

In eighteen hundred and sixty-seven,

The King lies to us in bilingual.

16

This land of headaches is fertile.

    The murderer speaks any language.

When bribes don't do the trick, Lord Amherst

    Invents bacteriological

Warfare in seventeen sixty-three

    With bed sheets riddled with chicken pox.

If extermination won't do,

Assimilation executes.

17

Kill a man, undermine rights
    Of the matriarch, and soon
The gates of prison hell open wide.
    The lawn under our feet comes
From rape. That this occurs in
    America or Africa,
The lesson to be learned is
The homework for the kids of the rich.

18

My friend wails that hail is a cloud
    In his Eden. What production
To make of it all? What form? What matter?
    What technique to expect from this?
For what purpose? asks Plato.
    To imitate, answers Aristotle.
To be able to find pleasure
And of course educate ourselves.

19

I am a bad reader, bad writer.
    I speak all idioms badly.
My folks did not write much, and worked
    On a narrow and rugged land.
Their factories specialized in
    Peddling emigration en masse.
Those who stayed behind made sure to
Call their own our assets and stories.

20

I had to usurp language
    And garden temporarily.
Yes, I was taught to love and share
    Each piece of bread, each glass of wine.
I would offer you some water,
    But someone poured arsenic in it.
We might not like him, still Dante
Is hard to tackle on his field.

21

Byron, Shelley, Keats exult the cult.
　　　More than loving it, artists revere
This territory where my genes
　　　Come from. I am not alone to write it.
Tourists pledge their allegiance
　　　And repeat it without shame.
I admit, I wish I could live there.
Then truth knocks me on the chin.

22

Pound gave it his body and soul.
　　　Mussolini too. It is he
Who concocted nationalism that will
　　　Tear the last century apart.
Men and women are obsessed by
　　　Geography like god and language.
Be aware. Neither soil, nor tongue
Bars you from being who you are.

23

Da capo. All locations are there
    To scout and relinguish.
It hurts, damn hurts, yet no place should
    Become a mirage or a cage.
What defines self is otherness
    And life love: the more we covet
The less ardour is relished.
Not Italy. But the Italic.

24

I understand, I don't understand.
    This upsurge lifting me to the unknown
Has no explanation. Imagine:
    A solution for everything.
What a bore if we could explain being.
    Nobles have no use for hermits,
Despised by right-thinking beggars.
A single hand can never clap.

25

Italian slaves filled suitcases
    With their crafts and skills, ran away.
Parallel kingdoms belong to
    No one, to everyone, to nothing.
Hope is the home of the outcast.
    Statesmen are dealing everywhere.
Sweet wine soon turns to vinegar.
Swindlers have no time for poetry.

26

I raise my glass to you, dear friend.
    Without accent, in solitude,
Content, blessed by comradeship,
    Music inside our body,
Our key for the gates of all cities,
    A promise of trade and respect.
I climb on my horse, wave good-bye.
A change of sky, a change of stars.

The Beginning

The first thing to do
Is to tear down his belief system,

Purchase this knave an ocean.
Undress him like an accordion.

Scrutinize his outdated pranks
And fashions piled up in his nest.

Roll over his sweat-coloured skin.
Run your fingers over his world solid as a skeleton.

Tug at his muscle ambition,
And pray that he won't imitate King Lear's daughters,

Nor Dante swaggering in his sugar-coated Inferno,
Nor Maldoror trudging with his suicide ghosts.

Freed of his religions and ideologies,
The irrelevant man lets himself coast

On the Tiber of his non-dreams
Like a bottle cast in a black river.

He opens his eyes to the screen
That begins with the word END.

He wanders through the white spaces
Between the alphabet of windows

And the sheaves of peacefulness.
This is the quick of his beingness.

What he wishes to learn
Is everything he can ever think of learning.

Light forms of beauty.
Frozen water of time.

Night siesta. Insomnia.
Rejection of the binary system.

The stars surface
From the sea, like happy bathers,

To breathe in the turquoise afternoon,
And dive into the summer waves.

Thermidor. Upheavals.
The public secret tears out the night

From his face and throws it
Into the pleasures of the fall.

But there is no fall.
The body sinks into the sky

That is an orange Earth.
His wings catch fire.

On his back a tattoo
Invites your caress.

All these pages.
All these faces.

All these teeth.
All this aggression against a friend.

The people and their setbacks.
The rules for the spectacle of hate.

These body portions diced as medals.
These engines deaf to the pilgrim.

In a couple of hours his ashes
Will be snow in your shower.

Days gather.
Achievements too.

The portals open.
The portals shut.

Windows open.
Shut, open, shut.

Sugar turns sour.
Salt spicy.

On the capsized mountain
Geography melts.

The breeze awakens the liquid rose.
Vanity forgets. Doubt astounds.

The sky brightens,
Ahead of his footsteps,

The berm running
Along the road is shorter

Than the path taken.
He picks up a dead leaf

And buries it in aluminum foil.
He is glad to be here where leaves sleep.

He is proud.
Today is a red night birth.

He leaves Venezia.
He returns to San Sebastían.

He starts from Mont-de-Marsan.
Crosses Toronto.

Now he is in Tallinn.
Udine Trier Zurich Trieste.

What to do with this Baroque identity?
Buon viaggio.

He spreads himself, gives birth to himself.
He is everything, and in this nothingness

A woman notices him on the train.
She tastes him with her sponge tongue.

There are orchids on her open blouse.
She begs the young man to sniff

And put his joyous lips there.
Will she apply agnus castus on their umbilical chord?

Two-Headed Man

He reads night and day.
His memory is a well.
On his iris, history reflects
The people on his block.

His mouth erects an ana.
His hands are shaped like a chrestomathy.
No, he is not a book lover.
He is a donkey.

His asceticism is an adventure.
His archaic skull shines
On a metal proof sheet.
He gets easily bored.

He moans like an alphabet box.
A mantra carries him to sleep.
He refuses relaxation.
If he nods

It is to caricature
The caribou and the oak tree.
Dreams, cluster of branches,
Open up to a river bed.

He plagiarizes the gods,
Grinds blessed images,
Sterilizes metaphors.
Slags spread over the desert.

Mirrors name him.
His mind crashes against the tinfoil
And cracks in two.
The dichotomy crowns him.

Straight lines curve.
His belly is a circle.
His nose sags.
His thoughts are pulled by mud.

Stuck in sludge,
He kowtows
Before the halo
Glow on his chair.

Blemish darkens his muzzle.
A lampoon against him.
He multiplies himself.
He is in everything.

The Futile Man

Here he stands with her cold tool.
Ready to lend it a voice, he who no longer
Has a voice, she who has such a pretty voice.

What use is it that she repeat to him
That in a break-up there is always
One who suffers more than the other?

He is once more the blackout.
He is skidding on a term
That is not synonymous with knowledge.

Every move he makes is an error.
Blinded by obsession
He cannot dictionary himself.

She lays her absence naked on the table,
This absence all round
She hands him like a fault.

She accuses him of mistaking fiction for reality,
Of being unable to see the world for what it is.
His eyes see well, his mind deciphers

The unrealities he is scared of losing.
She accuses him of mistaking madness for illusions.
His defects drive her crazy like his hammers.

The pounding behind the house
Echoes in her mind, a pulsing
That thrust her against tree skulls.

She sees life for what it is, for what it is not,
Tormented by the hubbub
Of his red car flitting.

Her nape tattoo accepts
His voice dropping from her cellphone.
A rock lifts her above and beyond

The projects crushed by his feet.
He, a friend, a cloud,
A jaguar beheads a paca

At the threshold of the ravished continent.

Zombies

*We have been made in such a way
that we forget that we were not made free.*
Paul Valéry

Zombies: a big hole where there once was a heart.
A row of shadows shuffle towards the poet's altar
Where he signs the one and only book they can read.
Behind his blue and white photo the same photo.
On the tables plates of potatoes with brown sauce.
No one smiles, no one weeps, taciturn all.
Monotonous music rhymes with his yes.
Above, no sun, no moon, no star, darkness.
Dancers sway through the walls, strut in unison.
Every man stares, hypnotized, no one speaks.
And then one laughs, and they all laugh.
The face in the mirror, the neighbour's face.
On the cracked tongue the cracked tongue of cousins.

Pier 21: Welcome

Every day I make my way through customs.
I first came here on May 1st, 1913.
Again on January 21st, 1930.
A third time on December 10th, 2000.
I love to travel, i.e. travel becomes me.

Where I come from where I am going
Is of no importance to boy or girl.
Sure, I help with the tribe's existence
In building its homes on fertile land
Where we erect our statues and gardens.

I also demonstrate with gangs that cut
Across the rich green fields of wheat
And blacken the summits with our arms,
Our tools, our fruits, and our women.
As far back as I can remember, for

Every man that leaves, another returns.
Land, no use reminding me, I know
Land land land never belongs to anyone.
Never anywhere do nomads take
The same trajectory twice from start to end.

I often meet wandering men who,
Like me, hop on a train bound for elsewhere.
I am a weak man who erases my steps
And begins life anew against all odds.
I am a convert who learns the native parlance.

I am a stubborn man glad to be stubborn.
I am counting the pennies that carry me
To the shores from which the ocean liner leaves.
I am the man horde, minus the conversion trauma.
The stateless man without a passport.

I sell identities, have no fondness
For language, no nostalgia, have no fear
Of abandoning home, mother, father, region.
Where I am I sing my difference,
My indifference, my wealth, my poverty.

And you, who are a warrior, who spurn
Exile, you extol hatred and prejudice
In another, who with a hundred fingers
Caress relatives you should not marry, beware:
Passengers, aboard, we are about to leave.

09.11.03

His suitcase, but suitcases no longer suffice
To contain the proposals he has folded within.

The end is in front of him,
Doodles on tablecloths he can't read.

Sand thickens on his glasses,
Embers of fugitive shadows.

No gin to slacken his muscles.
No fire to swallow for he can't get drunk.

Whiff of green, transitive painkiller.
He packs the suitcase he has just emptied.

Where to Go

I preludi del devenire.
Giorgio Vigolo

Where does he go to meet his friends?
The guy has spent most of his time
Running to bars where one hopes
To see a girl friend, a chum to share
The wine of friendship, a plate of pasta,
Nuts, peaches, invented arguments.

Italians are complainers, he says.
But if they moan today about
Some backache or some nastiness
On the part of the boss, it is to
Laugh about it tomorrow.
Neither the past, nor the future counts

For the worker who disputes the present.
At once a hedonist and a stoic,
This clerk quibbles with the little
He culls in the palms of his hands.
The books that fall from his lap
He uses to catch the better of the day

That plagues him. No Bible can
Disrupt his reveries.
He is not the romantic type.
No nice photography, no pretty images.
Just necessary images and photography.
He is allergic to the vain playwright

Who says evil people are illiterate.
Education does not guarantee
Generosity. History gives us
Few intellectuals for the Commune.
What is playful pleases. The hollow
Actor moves with arrogance.

Our poet envisages refinement.
Vision, even if vulgar. There are
Gestures that reveal graceful intent.
Psalms do not conceal their authors.
His bookie believes what
Has been written comes from the dieties.

This man is part believer, part atheist.
For the pagan preacher gods come from the fields.
After investigation and dialogue
Between heaven and hell, between sea and wind,
Supper for his candid family is served.
Solitude he has met too often is a talker

Who leaves him cold. He prefers teenagers in
The piazza. Contradictory community.
The hand that is most like his hand
Leads him away from love of self.
To read what he finds within annoys him.
Not the echo, but abandonment.

The blue jay soars over his walls,
Flying out of his fingertips. Enjoyable.
Irritable. Their somersaults, an obligation.
Gorillas raise a mirror
With imperfect silvering, for what
The poet calls Correspondence.

Back to Square One

The earth is a man, you say.
But a man is not the earth.
Octavio Paz

The man would like to start at the beginning,
    Because all beginnings are ambiguous,
Ambiguous because a beginning
    Is nothing else but a starting point.
It might be a semblance, a ghost,
    A dimension not well understood, a doubt.
To say that he was born here, in this city,
    Does not break his link to history
Passed down to him, traditions are not stories
    Told on farms where one refuses to acknowledge
Its citizens, its regions where artisans do
    Not speak the idiom of palm trees.
How to explain such a break, such a tearing,
    That is at once a wound and an offering?
A gift that a loving devil hands to a god
    Incapable of offering back love.
How can he discuss love and stay calm?
    Without raising his shoulders,
Without yelling, without shedding a tear,
    The man loves a divinity who does not love him.

He gives her his love at birth, a total love
        Destined to no other earthling,
A love that should always be a mistake
        For he never says no, never turns the key
Of the doors to the house locked to passers-by.
        Oracles walk through the doors torn by storms,
Tales of kindness and flawed love,
        Illicit love, illegal love, a love that
Does not imitate the indifference of Lords and Nations.
        The insignificant man loves with a love
That serves no purpose. Yet this love that serves
        Neither rogue nor idol has the power to heal.
It is there, beyond prison-cages and the grey marches
        To the clouds without soil, dung or stone,
That the wise accomplish what the unwise do for no reason.
        The unreasonable intent that is of no use to
The dancers of song, to the singers of dance,
        To the flower from the duet in *Lakmé*,
To the man who can no longer give, especially
        To the man who is unable to view the sea
From where rises the useless siren who hums love-future.

26.07.02

We are driving through the city in a convertible.
Ashes still warm on our shoulders.
On the radio, "A Very Special Place" by Mariano.

The murder of Lennon behind us.
The murder of thousands behind us.
The towers not on firm ground.

We are guilty, sing the victims.
We have caught culprits, sing the hangmen.
We are killed, sing the others.

Certain words have been banned.
Others swell into nightmares.
Three in this sports car are speechless.

A star drops in the middle of Times Square.
They are selling its fragments for freedom.
A young man inhales the fumes from a hairspray can.

No one is weeping, no one is laughing.
All streets converge into a gutter.
The East and the West wait for the red light to change.

The Stranger Stammers

The stranger stammers like a coughing car.
He will not unwrap the clouds
And divide the sea in two.

He throws himself into the carbage bin of good intentions.
He is vegetation injured.
Has the tough skin that survived the war.

This is an excuse for him to turn his head aside
When a boy jumps in front of a subway car.
He yawns like an old Italian woman

Before her son dead-white in his casket.
He hands you a sad pebble. He was taught
To inhale where many drown.

05.11.05

Too many of us are in this van.
Three children, four adults.
It is summer, it is winter, it is summer.
It is the impossible season at the end of a journey.

The road lies across the river, which means we must
Cross over by foot like coureurs de bois.
On our shoulders we are carrying
The van taken apart, piece by piece.

The husbands walk in front,
The wives walk in front as well, and in front of us
There is snow. Or is it the desert?
On the radio, it is 1950.

There, within us, a temple.
And a beach, because water too
Loses its cool when nothing
Seems to work on land.

Where are you going? ask two women
Sweating in their swimming suits.
Towards the Pacific? They laugh at us.
The boardwalk has no end.

The children sleep, the girl friend's
Hand clasps his hand,
As he describes the horror
On the president's face thinning on the screen.

Banking accounts are terror-stricken
Like robbers caught on video
Now printed on the first page of the paper.
Days are wavering gulfs.

The children sleep. The future is
Smeared with chalk make-up.
Parents laugh about a word
Dyslexia rolls over the never-ending sentence.

The homework finished, another war begins.
The circus is too tiny to withstand
The fire ripping through the stoppled storefronts.
Everything's under control, repeat the pepper police.

The Pacific joins the Atlantic.
The Earth turns over on its rings.
The ice melts. Auks are thirsty. Happy the god
Who documents his horizon gone crazy.

Urbs aurca

The discovery of a city
begins with the discovery of self.
Ermanno Rea

Urbs aurea. Golden city. City made of gold.
The irrelevant man imagines a city different
From the city in its present state?

He is outraged as he stands here
Facing the urban reality he wants
To embellish with his imagination.

Between reality and his fancy
There surely must be a hole
He can run to. If so, where is it?

He wonders what he is searching for when
He fancies a superior city. This gossip and
Vagary implicates the government.

Bear witness against unsackable bureaucrats
Who force workers to vote for parties
Before allotting commissions.

An artist should never expect
Help from his peers. No city employee
Works without some pre-established notion

Of what is ecological gain.
Established. Legal. Between the shovel
and the wallet he visits the bank.

The useless man posits a city centre
Where financial institutions are
Transformed into barter counters.

But here falls the president's bomb
On the library where alchemists change
Silver and gold into fruits and vegetables

And how the young teach the elderly
To share unemployment insurance.
This man's pockets are filled with sand.

The asphalt is patched, the snow
Bulldozed into a TV box home.
He sleeps to forget the afterlife.

The paper flaps need to be unstapled.
His dreams are dreams dreamt by all.
No need for secrets of connecting masks.

Every peach, every onion with its sticker,
Its hour of death.
He slices the circle into square strips

Of joy, each with a beginning and an end.
He pours in seconds to measure time
Necessary to complete the journey

From start to finish. He staples
A price tag and scratches the price out
For temporary relief.

Those who conjectured on noetic linearity
Also invented coins and safes
That contain metal scraps and value.

Hero removes the hands from clocks
And invites foreigners to his garden.
The opposite of saving accounts is dissipation.

Together they remove the negative
Connotations of skin, bone, and deposit boxes.
They transmute themselves and begin to glow.

Not so much with the alchemy of fraud
As with the flourishing of love.
Altruisim more than whim.

He who owns the keys to locks and doors
Yanks open the hooks that hold up the partition
Where a customs guard wears a golden crown.

Beyond the panel is a market where a girl
Exchanges zucchini flowers for a camera
And the spectators sit and watch

The juggler musician wandering by.

Exile

Every woman, every man, every second,
A needle between thumb and index,
A hammer in the hollow of the hand,
Fingertips on the handle bar,
Logos of wishes flashing through the clouds,
Every day, every girl, every boy
Meets this curse dropped
From the sky onto the body.
This private banishment is collective.
Not to flinch would produce unease, panic.
Pasquale Tarasco pulls a waltz out of his accordion
On the corners of Cuvillier and Hochelaga.
Agrocities are alike everywhere.
The paths, furrowed by the boots
Of Signor Raspa, his mule has trampled on
For a thousand years. Sarcastic hatching.
The breeze works its emotional havoc.
Do not divide our mulberry fields in two,
Cries the Pizzi family, on their knees in church.
The landowner in the meantime undresses Ilda,
Naive gatherer of eggplants.
The pig abounds in the master's trousers.
Do not wince, no. Yes, do wince.
The olive tree bends under the pressure of indecisions.
The bulge is no small feat

Before the goddesses of poverty.
Fast food slow food no food at all.
Vittorio and Carmine's departure
Has turned Gino into a rich man at the station.
Much more than bricks on his backs.
Everyone's story ignored by everyone.
The workman's milk spreads into a star
On the tablecloth, and without working papers,
The constellation waits to be named.
Saturday weddings are wanted,
Multicoloured, the widow's kiss diaphanous.
Breaking windows might be a welcome,
Sings the song of protest rising from the porch.
Repeat it, yes, repeat it, no, as you wish,
For there are criminal heads the size of cantaloups.
Ciciri, change your surname.
Ciciri, the Vespers scream.
Ciciri, vendetta's switchblade.
With such injustice,
With such a policeforce of lawyers,
With counterfeit tickets,
Giacomo counts himself lucky
To be among the living in prison.
On his face someone drew a large D in red.
Sixty percent of land
Belongs to 113 families.
Exile, the serf's modus vivendi.
Angelo is frightened of those
Who never fly south for the winter.

Mario tries hard to catch Maria's glance.
In the end both get bored of their eyes
They memorized for not looking.
Beware of couples that
Never leave their homeland.
Adamo's surprised there aren't more
Nomads on planes.
Run out quick, donate to charity.
Organize vagabond transportation.
Public faith crushed
By sham truths stuttered in alleys.
Dissension becomes impossible.
Every girl, every boy mistakes
The home for a blessing.
The neighbour steals computers viewed
Through the clothes hanging in the sunlight.
Let us leave our cottages.
Let us exchange passports.
Let the wind roll its wave
That will not sink
In the quicksand of privilege
For the native born.
Let us jump on our horses.
Let us climb aboard our ships.
Let us breathe
When suffocation begins.

To F., in memoriam

Violence inflicted violence befitted?
How did you ever break into
The barred gates of the forbidden?
This black blacker than black funereal.

To disappear to reappear
On the bottom page of news
Where the reader salivates
On your face in a forged passport.

Two against one makes four, but you,
Mathematician without a diploma, knew that.
Each with a gun in his jacket,
Death wins against three gangsters.

Intellectual of crime. *Et tu, Brute?*
Wailing from brother and sister. No priest
Has heaven in his rosary beads. Comatose,
Your mother's lament: *When can I see my son?*

Who teaches us to grind the blade
That groans into our neighbour's belly?
This community dims
Behind the sunglasses of murder.

The railing leads to the basement.
You can tell they are cousins
By their reserved demeanour.
Eyes lowered, they pull the blood curtain.

A celestial statue holds out her hand to you.
Everyone's an angel with black wings.
This afternoon is a prison hell.
Where is the soul for the rented body?

Fingers reach out to the impossible.
Eyes scrutinize what must not be viewed.
Judas is as sure as Cain
In the unfolding of this narrative.

The plot begins with its ending.
You against the wall, holes in your heart.
A dozen bullets made of solid gold.
Please don't pretend it don't hurt.

Click, click, click, screams the rival.
Fire, fire, fire, laugh the paparazzi.
The X of the unschooled chant
A prayer about the vowels of clouds.

Don't you dare grin Surprise.
Each gesture brought you to this grave.
Terrible is our family love
Erect before your spirit in debt.

Daughter

Figlia,
Sospiro pubblico,
Papa loves the roaring of your lions in flight.

A Father, a Daughter

Her day. Wake up at six-thirty.
His daughter, up already, climbs up
To his bed, slips in.
Let's go have breakfast, Papa.

Hand in hand, they fly down the stairs.
From the third floor bedroom to
The second down to the first floor.
The door is a nimbus.

He fetches the dishonest newspaper
To keep abreast on his enemies.
Read whatever shrewdness
People who hate can come up with.

Cereal into a bowl for the little one.
He poses for Elisa busy drawing.
He eats a glass of water and drinks
Two slices of bread and gruyère.

They wash and jump
Into the station wagon.
Eight o'clock, on the dot, they run to school.
They hum hello to Mses Fugère and Doyon.

He kisses his daughter, dragging her wings.
Drives back, and coughs water
On the porch as he prays to the trees.
A cat barks in the park and leaves.

Quiver in the yellow breath of a dead god.
He creeps in the room and slips into the computer.
The day berserk with creditors' yelling.
He escapes when he picks up his daughter

Savoring a slice of mozzarella-tomato
Pizza. On the radio, rap
She knows by heart. Late supper.
They discuss a film and start to dream.

At night, the father turns sleep into work.
His head scrambling through old regrets.
A racoon walks up to the child's window.
The moon lowers its green paw on her pillow.

09.04.02

To Louis Dudek

His daughter is taller than his mother.
He teaches her about ocean horses.
The Arctic icecap melting.
He could cut a piece of the sky
And blow it into her lungs.
What good would that do? She knows that.

People love singing conspiracy rhymes
Instead of learning about the benefits of ignorance.
This is the great paradox, isn't it?
The more one knows oneself
The more one loses oneself in a collectivity.
Each community must burn its flag.

Poets love the monarchy, oblivious
Of the trowel that built museums.
The father reads Victor Hugo, convinced
That imitation is the opposite of loving.
His daughter prompts him about how gold
Must fold under the weight of pain.

Springtime, and the earth slumbers.
Respect prefers we do not vote.
Sunset voices are lengthy shadows
That blue jays turn to fire.
We will never be tall enough
For the modern age.

The Devil Does Not Want

The devil does not want her evil being.
He wants to walk beside her on the boulevard.
His manners are no different than hers.

The rock between them, why destroy it?
The dancing step they are learning to dance,
Why bother to put an end to it?

He confesses his future mission to her.
Why pay for groceries alone? The rent
Alone? He can help. He holds her hands.

He can grow from day to day, with her.
Without her, he cannot get to his destination.
Do not rip to shreds my words. He is shivering.

Lugging around from one side to the other,
His fingers toilsomely
Turning the key to her room.

He undoes her bed.
How to appreciate another's culture?
How to revel in her foreign embrace?

They are distressed. They are
Frightened of one another. He believes
She hates him, and she, that he hates her.

He recounts the time he bellowed his hatred
To her, reminds her how, night
After night, she screamed *I hate you*.

After allowing him to make love to her.
I hate you. What does he make out of hatred?
Fabulations. Can you say why you love me?

He sees her for who she is. He is naive,
Curious, intense, nervous. He notices
The wings on her back unfolding.

Your Body

This olive-coloured landscape
I never expected to touch
Becomes rigid when breathing
Is quick and pleasure wild.

You're what no northern light reveals.
The other side of the moon and sun.
The nectar you give me to drink
Is darker than whiskey and joy.

30.05.12

The sun plummets down to earth.
A girl of fifteen
Is eating a pear, and the rest is
A story about a broken family that
Is quite out of the ordinary, for
Right there before the end-wall
Grief changes into an exit.

The Nightmare

The nightmare that shook me up fades.
I return to life reading James Baldwin.
The geraniums on the balcony have more vitality
Than we two tonight. Endings, transformations

Are themes we need not fear. Each decision,
Its moment. You are cutting asparagus, inhaling
Nervously: *I hate your puns.* Is reason
A harbour? He who deprecates the other

Deprecates himself. Our contract
Is an enigma without solutions. We will
Evaporate like methane before we

Can pay back all we owe. Power is
Control of self, and we can scarcely
Control the knobs on our stove.

Night Drive

The road is dizzy with raindrops.
I forgot to turn on the light.
It's night everywhere down here.
Never thought I'd blow a fuse.

    I'm cold, not sure that's true.
    When was it I could think straight?

Feels like I shouldn't drink and drive.
Don't recall when last we spoke right.
No phone connects me to you.
All we owned broken at your feet.

    Teach me the ways to say I love you,
    Even if it is make believe.

        It's time, time to come home.
        Time to praise the sun
        You are to me.

Nothing seems to matter anymore.
I once was rich now I'm poor.
Who cares what crime I might have done,
You'd rather see men like me run.

Some days we'd have broken down the door.
Today we left love hurting on the floor.

It's time, time to come.
Time to praise the sun
Love is for us.

18.05.02

To Herménégilde Chiasson

A cardinal sings my awakening every day.
By sunrise I have deciphered the meaning of its song.
Never monochord, its sounds reveal their puzzle
And how melody too can become a stutter.
The stench of chalk is as imposing as electric wiring.
Wrapped around a neck, a mistake can be a truth.

The mystic's shudder or the delinquent's grenade.
The aristocrat has no use of kings and queens.
Every mariner meets the mayor of every port.
The ambidextrous loner is an all-rounder.
Master of guitars that I foolishly try to tune,
Will you not come and help me forge a song?

The outsider hunts and, partner in crime, smiles.
No bird refrain is free of its crackle.
I learn to listen to the sea before running,
To sleep before flying into the sunrise.
On motherlands, on nativelands,
I paint staying put by escaping.

Uprooting

To pull out from the ground.
Man blubbers, therefore he falls.
He uproots himself and makes a beeline for
The edge of the precipice with the idea
Of throwing himself off in order to soar away.

First to eradicate himself from his country.
Again, he's not quite sure from which country,
Nor from which ground. A poor metaphor,
Indeed, to capture the skyfish or the sparrow
He's become scuttling on the sea floor.

To pull himself out of his glebe, his nucleus.
Simon Weil writes that the family
Where he finds loving no longer
Matters. Without glebe or family
Where can he run to now?

He has done what he could to change
The rootless man into a myth, by
Dressing him in noble attire worthy of princes,
And by tearing off his frock and guiding him
Naked into the lower depths of the city on fire.

Castoffs, rags, rings, dirty fingernails,
Each is free to cut the lawn on which
He saw light. The topsoil is cement
From which he cannot free himself.
The nation is a web for spiders

Playing with sticky nets on which
The caterpillar citizen is prevented
From developing into a butterfly.
Total being has no place in this glade.
On middle ground, this victim

Receives a spell that the devil casts on him.
Mistakenly. Both are too drunk
To see that the wrong man has been chosen.
Our futile man analyses the circumstances
And pries himself out of the glue.

But no pill is capable of killing
His headache. No. Yes. There is a hole
In his skull, right there, in the back of his head,
The size of a silver coin, and it is through
That metal that a cool blast

Lifts him up from the muck,
Elbows him to his knees. He
Grabs hold of a branch, but his fingers
Rend and his fists sap.
He lets go, and he drops down

Fast, his fingers painfully
Tear off and, one nail at a time,
He slackens his grip, keels over,
Carried by the updraft supernatural.
There are no cheers to be heard when

The spectacle of the great collapse ends.
The man finds himself far up
The stream. He wedges his bleeding
Hands into the sand, holding on to a root
He tries to move up to the stage.

Unable to perform his part, he
Takes a deep breath. His heart is wide enough
To carry the family he won't leave behind.
He tightens his lips, refuses to breathe.
It is a trick he had learnt as a child.

His body starts to swell,
His heart balloons. There
Are no teardrops on his cheeks.
No handkerchief can absorb the water
Flowing like from a plastic container

Tipped over. And the water turns into
A river which runs to the ocean,
Where his feet feel free,
Propelling him up, as his shoes slip off.
The afterward becomes here-and-now.

This man has no regrets, no yearning.
He flies from town to town
Without snapping off a piece of his being.
The truth is, and it is his truth,
He's inept at losing whatever he stuffs

In his heart bag. Aspirations. Inspirations.
Missions. Never a loner, always alone,
He's a weak man who like any stranger is
Thankful for whizzing as he pleases.
He notices his legs can transmute

Into a garden of shooting stars.
Trees and flowers of every kind blossom.
The fig fruits as big as tomatoes
And branches as awkward as vine
Climb up, crawl across brick walls

That extend and encompass the sun.
The uprooting disturbs no colleague.
The refusal to settle down is
What troubles the boss. Who speaks?

He eschews dwelling of permanence.
Doctors tell him rootlessness is
Sickness fit for museums, entertainment
For traitors. Roots are vital.
The kernel is absent. He's a coward.

The seed stolen by robin and crow
Drops from beak to sod.
Reckless orioles are spoilers.
The thicket is starving. He darts out.
Pelicans pour fire water on his lawn.

By capsizing in his orchard, he,
The gardener, turns his back to the sky
Blessed by carrier pigeons. Eagles
Reveal how parting is not as tough
As the absence of a resting place.

Intruder

The sense of being no one among lost ones.
André Roy

The intruder smooths land surface
Like sandpaper of time-desert.

He yelps for help in his nightday,
Friend of crosswind, enemy of mortar.

Papyrus of public thought,
Transmitter of epics by the worried mind.

The merchant's standard, the nobleman's good.
The future can harness his secrets.

More than a drooling monkey,
This offspring of survivors

Has the DNA of the earth worm.
A burden of parables embezzled from hamlets.

The decentralized centre.
Sacredness debunker.

In the literary salons of Naples,
His touch is a hand on the wall of prayer.

The welcome of seat and cupboard.
Restless legs know more than eyes,

Taste more than the tip of tongue.
A gift to unwrap for the devil at his door.

He flies to hell without drowning.
He dives into heaven's ballast without drowning.

He breathes more than the air he breathes.
No bottle in those lungs he calls person.

Freezes, pallid, in front of massacre.
Engages in logic to win lost causes. He proves

The axioms he patrols. He draws
The imprints he unravels. He reinforces

The wonders never become truths.
He wades in a grammar in the making.

He avoids falling into the depths of the galaxy.
He snatches happiness when sadness least expects it.

Beyond the breaking of what can never be broken.
Beyond moving forward with rearview mirror.

He accepts water, rock, wind, turf
And what flexes wave and sun of night.

The interloper unfastens the straps of straight-jackets,
Casts theorems of non-existence, and leaps away happy.

Interlude

Listening to the anarchist singing on the radio,
The reporter remembers the sneer on the editor's face
Who fired him for printing *piece of ass*
Instead of *piece of luck. But why?* the writer begged.
Don't both phrases mean one and the same thing?

The Universe Is Calling

The universe is calling. With its lower case upper case fingers
Reaching out for the plastic pouch in your womb.
With its sexes suffocating in your titanic sheaths.
It is demanding to be kneaded like dough.
Recognize me, it yells, it whispers, it listens, it is silence.
Constellations in your veins mirror its eye colour.
Muscular clouds of your thighs are its asteroid storms.
When it rains, you suns. When it smiles, you teardrops.
Its good manners deter you from conflict with yourself.
What privileges you? What laws you? What parties you?
The universe awakes at midnight and hauls you to midday.
On the highway it races you to yourself.
You fall asleep when Bach sings *Sleeps Awake*.
Here are your daughters you do not recognize.
Here are your daughters who do not recognize you.
The universe knocks at your door
But you do not speak its language.
There are subtitles everywhere but you cannot read.
Cramps crook you over, drugs excite your fears.
You run to the estuary of happiness.
On the moving walkway you slide back
As you make your way forward.
You bathe in the estuary of happiness
You mistake for the pilferer of souls.
The universe is calling, but you cannot hear.

Paris Is Far

Paris is far, so is Rodin's *Secret*,
Those lovers' hands that caress one another
Without touching, a whisper that encompasses what
Can't be confined, my home is a city of confinement,
Though the cage is invisible and the bars glittering.
Paris is a secret that unfolds within like a whisper.
The walls fall apart when the tax driver smiles
And the waiters laugh: This restaurant
Is a lover's sex for poets to kiss. What lips
Have we touched today? No price to fix
On the works the unknown promises.
In the atrium, workers of joy.
Above, the aristocrats of history snore.
One leaves, one gives, one takes, one breaks.
No photograph can capture the multi-dimensions
Of those fingers that touch without touching.
This street is a haven for replicas where touching is rebirth.

On Stage

On stage in a tavern a young immigrant
Accompanying himself on an orange guitar
Delivers more joy to the spirit than
The struggle for the survival of culture.

A boy throws a Molotov cocktail
At the foot of the crafty devil.
The bridge connects two deaths in red,
A refrain in his rhyme about love lost.

Horrible that the art of a country
Be in the tiny hands
Of one
Who promotes death.

The assassin and his paradoxes.
What is song is not song.
What he sees is less than sight.
A tractor rips the earth beneath our feet.

Meschin

Meschin watches *Scarface*, assimilated by paranoia.
Languishes deep in the sofa, trembles.

The autumn wind is a machine gun weeping.
He too has killed for a cause.

He crosses the path taken by the racist city
Counsellor who smiles at the policewoman.

Power pulls a wry face, shows its fangs.
The meschin is a vaudeville artist.

The masses enjoy him on the news,
Dedicating himself to goodwill misery.

Standing naked in court, he stammers.
This is the last time you see me alive.

Faith bursts like an abscess.
Blood squirting is no parenthesis.

It binds an idea to his brain.
He lives like a promise he cannot fulfil.

Raped for being different.
Executed for discordance.

The traitor's archives
Tumble down the garbage shoot.

He is Jacques Brel on the porch:
Oh to see your friend cry.

Meschin does not believe that your hand
Will not be the warm sun on his nape.

He is lost.
A recluse among many.

The Devil's Stiff Neck

The atom apple is the reason for his stiff neck.
The lost stranger's journey.
His hermetic life more crazy than visionary.
The robot joyfully welcomes trash as gift.
He invites us to his fat paradise.
His head twirling towards obsession.

A plot to exterminate nomads.
His snare drum for pre-birthing,
A monument for the racketeer's grave.
Slave, he makes a wish list of leftovers.
His echo, a mirror for the narcissist.
His photograph is overexposed.

He feels creepy but not guilty.
Intoxicated but not alcoholic.
In love but not blindly.
He is a birch tree that rakes in
The leaves forgotten by autumn.
No matter what he swallows

He is an animal thing, a male object.
He is stalker, he is hatred, gnashing teeth.
He is bashing of immigrants.
He is thumb-nose laughter, road rage.
He is vein melting under prick of needle.
He translates plagiarism.

He is anorexic warrior with gun and sword.
He is man against the unknown.
He is disapproval of prayer. He orders murder.
He is manifesto for wretchedness.
Nothing rhymes with his blood.
His bawling is betrayal is switchblade.

Slicing the speechless womb of the enemy.
No noun, no adjective, no highway,
No fixed itinerary, no dead-end alley.
Chemistry marries biology.
Between his thumb and his contempt
The nomad splits like cheap jewellery.

To come together, to separate, to climb up
To epiphany, this man copulates with the monkey.
What is this guy? He mimics god the master.
Who cares about the cracked tooth of lies.
In front of castles, memory becomes monologue.
This is a soldier who can't remove his eyes

From the horse's rut, the blindfold of faith.
This creature has the scent of banners.
This man is breath stolen from burning flesh,
The fur in his mouth is human hair.
It all belongs to him: parallel trail
Torn off and insult of happy homecoming.

The Forest

Leni Riefenstahl dies at 101.
A reporter teases the German filmmaker

For not refuting her ideology.
Suicide vents itself in what is left unsaid.

Who among us shall be pilloried?
Who will defend innocence at the tree trunk?

Neither tree trunk in the forest fire,
Nor finger in the flame will be left unscathed.

Tomorrow our children will say
That we acted like Miss Leni.

What Does This Politician Want?

What does this politician want? A bed to sleep in.
A woman, or maybe a man to love.
To be cared for by. Friends.
To get drunk with. Power.

On TV men just like him, enemies.
Editors hunt down hired guns and their lovers.
Spectators screech. He is the strongest.
A lady flies in to free him from the rut.

A child. A child will never break
In front of those who know only hatred.
Companies and the military salute.

Today a picture of this dictator appears
In the paper. Tomorrow there will be
The photo of another dictator just like him.

Soldier

The soldier does her morning yoga.
In the afternoon, child womb and bowl.
She lights a reefer and caresses
The machine gun pointed at
Jews Muslims Christians Hindus.
Rumours advertise:
All bourgeois are racists.
The body is older than the mind.
She hammers a nail in your eye.
With her will and medals, she hollers *God is Me*.
One day we found her husband's corpse
In a field of clover marked: *Dispensable*.

An Aside

A succubus died to meet the soldier.

Heavy breathing at the end of the line.

Verbal maundering, fingertips on ankle.

When the husband fell asleep.

When the spouse fell asleep.

Stealthy looks, blue hydrangea.

Standing Behind Death

Standing behind death a prankster adlibs.
An aria from *La Bohème* by Puccini.
May the gods pay no regard to him.
Spicy red peppers hang in the sun.
From East to West, it is all the same.
In every eye, the green light of contentment.
Pop open the champagne waiting at her feet.
A wink is an elephant's lie.
Memory flickering, memory fluttering.
Who are we tonight on this rooftop,
Mesmerized by Chinese fireworks,
Embracing our love for never?

Prima donna

Ruth, she remembers it well.
Katrina? Impossible, she's a saint.
Sara, never, now a red-head, she lives in Siberia
With Alice who is studying the sensuality of glaciers.
Misty, she got to know one.
Oh yes, Felice takes herself for truth incarnate.
Clarisse had suicide twins called Nation and Nation.
Georgia points her finger accusingly.
What right does she have? Esther loves hers.
Charity has no idea what to do with her finger
When it is her turn to touch her kitty.
(Dear, that rhymes with sexuality!)

Slammer or Licker

Are you a slammer? Are you a licker?
The questions put Don Juan's faith in tilt.

The devil steps into the wrong party.
The guests, the majority, raise two fingers.

The ladies grunt like raging bulls.

Carlo Silvio Orlando burst out laughing.
Santina Erminia Tina bite their smiles.

Eh, guaglio' se' nu romantico
of the domestic tabby. Ow ow ow.

The tongue is the poor man's cock.

We want our beds to roam
From room to room.

Girl Friends

The girl friends take a flight down South.

The heat is a contradiction.

Confidence is the fertilizer for palm trees

Growing in the Alps.

Surpassing Jupiter.

The two women argue.

Neither wants to miss the devil glancing back.

Like Setsuko Hara

Like Setsuko Hara in the foreground,
The classiest of guests,
Her dress needs no adjectives,
Her smile needs no silk,
She primes on-lookers to love.

Turn off the cameras.
Dig up the basil.
Where she will learn
To steady her balance
Without the help of a kite.

Cleopatra and Anthony

Cleopatra did not love Anthony
The night she asked him:
Must I give back to you
The country I conquered?

He, face half shaven.
She, face upside down,
Keeled over by the general's last caress.
A star lands on her blue orange.

Fellini defines the confines
Of consciousness
As being a sea that separates
The before and after of childhood.

Cleo conceals her night,
Her head beneath the bed sheets.
Three in the morning,
Stooges walk out of the walls.

How many times must she
Slip on her gloves to cross a mirror.
Her life is a musical comedy
With climaxes and denouements.

She wobbles on the parapet,
Delighted as an overturned couch.
She shuts her umbrella
And dances in the rain.

Listen to how the Earth
Has stopped turning.
Cleo pulls the arm of the clock
One way, and Anthony, the other.

Casanova

Casanova leans on the counter like a waitress,
Fiddling his long hair, antsy, eager
For clients, aware how the service imparts

Integrity to he who rattles pennies
In the cup, his fingers, fidgety, next to
The ash tray dulled by half-smoked

Cigarettes, a rancid droplet of sweat
Without special connotation,
A spoon, a knife slid under

The paper napkin, the back page of a novel
Clouded by tea knocked over
As he is knocked over by the ray of light

Striking the shoulder of your jacket,
A melody rising like a magic carpet
On which he'll waggle you for a price.

He will never say no to your silly grin.
He is space yearning for your touch.
You are hands greeting this space.

19.11.10

The wager, dreadful. The tornado intensifies.
A thousand policemen guard
The condos of couples in love.

They accuse the speechless man
Of stealing strangers' words
To soil the tribe's mother tongue.

The target minus the target,
The unimaginable minus
The unimaginable.

Everywhere, a nowhere. The intent, dubious.
A victim is a conjecture
When black turns grey or white on white.

The man does not speak of a god but a horse.
Of a time when the zebra disapproved of its stripe,
When cats praised wild dogs for not eating cows.

16.02.06

Politics is a plate of meat gone bad.
On every flag, a drop of blood.

On every mask, a realization.
The fanfare whets the confidence of the roar.

Here the 0. There the 1. Tomorrow dead. Good riddance.
A mortgage a child can never pay.

The devil speaks. A beep for every word.
A digital program for every warfare.

Each his paintbrush. Each his cannon. Each his rocket.
Each his pledge to his undertaking.

The oil stain on the Pacific rises in his veins.
A man rips off his face.

23.05.01

Gone for good the great eye.

Friends of youth, graves of greenness.

A gap where once a tooth shined.

Don't remove the circumference of the world.

God is a generalization.

What a Wonderful Day

To Fulvio Caccia

What a wonderful day to kill yourself.
You can enrol in the armed forces,
Tie a bomb to your thigh, spill tons
Of crude oil into the river where
A million fish foxtrot night and day.

Better still, let the river sway like fish,
Dilute the oil with water, toss a salad,
Untie the bomb, recycle the metal,
Invite the army to clean the mess
Before raising your glass, a toast to life.

Whiteness

Whiteness blackens the warrior's dream.
Keen to forfeit desire and quench his gun thirst.
Dictionaries scorch with double entendre.

The devil warrants insurrection and hangings.
From priest to nun, the salesman of sermons.
Annihilation is easier than patience.

Loving more disconcerting than destruction.
The gangways lead to holes and perils.
The vanishing point won't carry him home.

The chaconne fades to a pause
In his main artery and turns to liquid.
Milk swindles his babies born, his babies killed.

To stop war he should sing out loud,
Refrain from eating his bird of paradise.

She Says

We must do it, she says, for the dreaming spirit.
For the non-loved one, for the unthinkable.
Is she weeping or simply forgetting?
Our girl cries: *Don't divorce.*

Between she and she a chasm where family slips out.
A den where she runs to hide herself.
She unspools, as her world begins to spin.
Werewolves howl: *Down with freedom.*

A ravine as wide as a foundation,
A slide,
A sprig
Flourishes where grass could never sprout.

On water in water by water,
What flows, what flows back, a cuckoo, a buzzard,
A tube deflates, an air balloon rolls
Onto the prickly bramble of good cheer, bursts.

The Suns

Carefree he who meets with
The split half of himself.
Content he who heartens
Society with his single love.

There will be days when
Disdain will be constant,
Nights when handshakes
Turn to hand grenades.

When what is inside dries brittle.
When what is outside chips.
The hearth you built yesterday
Will need repairing.

It is the rival suns that brighten
The gloom of our demons.

Plagiarized Poem

Mouth, do not speak, be quiet.
Do not voice the sweetness of love.
Do not whisper of heart and its rapture.
Mouth, do not say love
Knocks at your door,
Nor pipe the pain your lips can harbour.

Broccoli

Cauliflower and Rapini have a child in 1560.
Better known as the vulgar town idiot,
Broccolo decides it be best to emigrate.
Gossip has it that language deprives him
Of alphabets that leave him without a face.
Some say he has not been the same since.
Others accuse him of simple play acting.

Like the tall and gentle Jacques Tati,
He is stuck looking down at his friends. Sure
Of himself, without a trace of pride or scorn,
He is a homeless child living in a box,
In every city, in every country.
Never clumsy, a polyglot,
He breathes through deformed fingers.

He stands in front of the customs officer.
Dogana corrects his name with her pen.
A few centuries alone behind the counter,
The woman invites him to supper.
From peach fuzz to man with newfound self,
A hundred boys and girls rush out
Across the fields of broccoli.

Riddles

1

because he's here
means he's there

but what good
where he's from

if after saying so
he replies *when?*

does he know what to
be or how to come when

smitten with who's
being elsewhere

saying why he's
gotten here

before having
left there?

2

does the devil
like it

if the enemy
doesn't prick
his meat?

3

will the Earth
come back

harmless
from the Moon

when everyone's
out for a stroll

each with
his subtitles?

4

his face?
his laughter?
you know who he is.
his handcuffs?
your pleasure?
you are he.

5

if
it
breaks
on
earth
who
will
fix
it?

heaven?

Insomnia

The night is never kind.
Its pockets are filled with suns.

Taxi

Rings, ballerina shoes, woolen skirt: she.
Isn't this all he could hope for?
A feeling of contentment.

He understands, she orders, they enjoy
The same melody, the same cacophony.
Respect laws to a tee and the State collapses.

They ridicule the stance
Taken by the passably educated judge.
They blow the horn on the referee.

The lovers discuss, as tourists do,
Stepping out of the airport, pulling suitcases,
Unable to decide which direction to take.

A secret sentence vibrates in their presence.
Love that loses itself in a taxi
Kills them with its geography.

Hollywood, Florida

Where to spend the rest of one's life?
Stephen Vizinczey

Hollywood, Florida, my feet do not touch the ocean floor.
Way past my mid-life crisis, I who wanted to be blonde,
Am whiter than grey, fatter than thin, my daughter
More woman than teenager, my lover more dough than yeast.
The sun bores red holes into our skin. Close to noon.
The Atlantic turns over on its back, sprawls on the beach.
Many years ago a woman stuck a needle into my belly.
I am cursed, my family knows that I've got bad luck.
The moon is white and round, the sky burning and blue.
A shark blacker than lava rubs itself against my foot.
Who would have guessed that inspiration comes with handcuffs?
Ringing in my left ear. Someone speaks nicely of me.
Happiness stretches on the hot sand, stares at a woman
Parading her rococo in her splendor to men with eyes
Larger than balls fit for endangered species. Laughter.
Yelling. Kites at the tip of young Cubans' fingers.
Ex-patriots. No talk of politics on this holiday.
A romantic poet with a camera takes a shot of a lady,
Suntanned, describing how floats to her toes a suicide.

Bob Dylan

Bob Dylan, the poet?
My mind wanders back to Robert Burns,
Famous for his requiems dedicated to his Nordic peoples.
I think of Homer, Virgil. I hear the anxiety
Of men and women in their murmuring.
I hear Léo Ferré, Georges Brassens.
You insist that poetry is Stéphane Mallarmé, Nicole Brossard.
But it is also Paul Verlaine and Leonard Cohen.
I raise my glass to the poetry of song.
Not my intent to reduce poetry to rhyming verse,
Nor condense it to a list of impressive names.
I testify to a rhythmic syntax of effigies
That jump outside margins anchored by concepts,
Paper scribbled by ink for the pleasure of eyes only.
Song imitates the glorious everyday voices
Of daughters, sisters, mothers, and fathers.
I envy the poet who blends music to painting.
Words bend with his salutary bow that delivers,
In the emergency room of scorn, love unleashed.
No light shines immediately. Doubt questions facility.
Syllables refuse to stay imprisoned to a keyboard.
The voice trips out, breaks, develops into an image.

It is fiction fused with the heartbeat of society.
When I listen to Zimmerman, I hear telluric chanting
Crash against the indifference of the sky.
The most precious of moments is to awaken
To the singer's call for presence. And so
I swirl, joyous, under the influence
Of this blue-eyed bluesman,
Solace for my human stupidity.

At Last

At last the fragrance of manumission
Heralds the untamed season.
A man notices sweat seeping
From his pores, sticking to his skin.

Salt water reminds him that summer
Is energy oozing from simple things.
In his pyjamas, he opens the shades,
Slides the aluminum door, and invites

In the sun full force. His files
Get scattered across the studio by the draught
That ruffles what is left of his hair.

The breeze lowers its hand on his shoulder,
As he steps out of the prisons
Of winter and its procession of worries.

Amazonia

Let Amazonia be a nova in his hands.
Conflict celebrates life.
The demon runs amuck with want.
The tree is a pianist banging a dirty trick.
What does he offer if not phrases without punctuation
Blurry photographs bright kitchen lights.
The living room is a faint voice a candle
Asbestos stuck to his toes sneaking out.
She reminds him he is a figment of her imagination.

Handsome Man

The opposite of youth is not old age, but artificiality.
Jacques Tati

The man boy suffers from sleep disorders.
The young man has not slept in years.
Pipe dreams are smeared around his eyes.
His hands tremble after drowning
Rats pushing him off his security bench.

The chipmunk and the woodpecker argue
About the birch tree turning red or green.
Pediatricians detect apnea.
Vets diagnose anxiety.
Physicians have found no solution

For his planet growing in density.
For his sun shrinking.
For his plastic become food.
For the scarcity of oxygen
In his lungs too tiny to breathe.

For the man youth, everyone is seduction.
For the man old, happy if one is to his taste.
He traces his wounds on sand
And carves his joys in stone
That no wind will ever erase.

The city ceiling crushes the ash.
The high-rise welcomes UFOs.
The squall is the invisible.
The useless man sails through time layers.
His fingers tighten the levers of anti-memory.

The man twenty mistakes himself for a spirit.
The man thirty is a dust ball
In every corner of every room.
Killing the man forty is less expensive
Than allowing him to rob a bank.

His karma is grime on a penny,
Peat moss under his potbelly.
An auditor sits on the gurney
Where the man fifty recites his psalms.
Detectives accuse the weak man of fraud.

The fire dies, stars burst, sprinklers.
Circuits goes on strike. The mind blanks.
The lines on hands get wiped out.
Leisure sneers, the law shows its teeth.
The man sixty is a vaudeville artist.

He sees himself on the big screen. His caution,
The colour of hope. *The real condition*
Of man is to think with his hands.
The man seventy is damned.
The atheist lifts his forefinger

And presses on a gadget
On the naked shoulder, there, between neck
And blouse of his wife eating cancer.
The man eighty folds like fragility.
He spreads out like oblivion.

The corner-store clerk waits. The crook
Taps his foot. Reacts before action starts.
Reprisals for offensive.
Mountain of grief, skin insults skin.
The fork pokes the glass shattering.

Slivers of communion.

The man ninety, the sprain of Achilles' ankles.

The man unsure is ready to convert.

The man revelation faints in final slumber.

The man reincarnation undoes his nightmare.

Italian Alphabet

Attempt to survey the horizon
Better far than forever a
Certain vision grants
Due notice to more than less by
Eliminating the too large
Fallacy of praise
Grounded on men who
Hit men and other
Illuminated spectres and stone hearts
Lapidate guardians of
Memory vacated and replaced to
Negate indifference in helping
Poor boys poor girls with swollen bellies who
Quiver before eyes hidden behind cameras not
Responding shutting down calmly
So obesely so religiously in
Tourism meant for
Urbanity wrapped in sophism while
Visiting lords lie down and multiply
Zeros on the crowns of their serfs.

Dante

1

The grassland sorrows its vegetation. Wellspring
of Eastern fields and winter
pastures dozing in the evening.

An unfading book continues to unsettle us.

Et per consequens nec optimum vulgare.

The spring season has no culture, no talent.
The scrub has been forbidden
to speak its vulgar tongue.

Poor Dante, so many centuries spent
on lobbying your intransigence.

The shadow spreads over the garden red
                                    universal.

2

Customs are fixed by the pleb.
Machines emulate the human voice
to praise parent and child.

The era, a cellphone in spasm,
tells us of a friend who has passed away.

Cino da Pistoia and his companion:
the poet doctor delivers his address.

The turf is embarrassed.

Which is more important:
the dandelion or the rose?

The shadow waters the garden yellow

regional.

3

Where does the synthetizer go,
on which perfume of noise,
fanciful overflow of
this fragile season?

The foliage hisses. Evasiveness.
Nanar, wake up and dance to the music
of leaves brittle under our feet.

The shadow leaps
into the womb
                in bloom.

Spring perennial in our undertaking.
Spring brash in our laziness.

Allora Gino

And so, Gino, tell me what have we unravelled
In this brightness we were looking for?
Not that the luminance we left behind was
Darkness. Such a comment would be
In bad taste. Let us agree then that one
Never leaves a town for lack of light,
But for the quality of its light source,
For the virtual image which seems stronger
Than the glow from the candles
In our hands, we are like blind Tiresias,
Half men half women, with children,
Attractive, healthy, educated, by our side,
As we walk towards a large screen
Emptied of its convictions.
The wallets we find on trains
Belong to our grandfathers.
We express the obvious.
I have come to accept that departure
Is elicited neither by suffering nor politics,
But by biological necessity.
The unavoidable impetus towards
Imperative change.

The subtle pre-human drive towards
The unknown, towards what has no name,
Towards that moment of intimacy
Shared by lovers standing in the middle
Of a square in a foreign town.
To declare that yesterday was
Prison and today liberation
Would be a lie. Nothing more disturbing
Than the final hour that awaits us.
Yet here we are. Where, you ask?
I can't say. Here? I have no idea
What that means. By laughing,
By weeping we crossed
The river in one piece. Without affliction.
Don't ask me to describe this train station
Where we share a tea, a handshake, a good-bye.
We are where we are supposed to be.
Tomorrow is the step that follows the preceding step.
A gearing forcibly grinds forward
Regardless of our awareness or will power.
You pull open the shutters. Blackbirds greet
Your awakening with their good morning.
Alms are never a nuisance.
This is the price we pay when we choose
To embrace and welcome foreigners.
To procrastinate behind closed blinds
Sours a meal, turns wine to vinegar.
Listen to soldiers thundering for us not
To touch the brick of the sacred wall.

Between the wrapping and the tile
A hole through which friends confer.
Chatterboxes bicker at sunset.
Impossible for them not to recognize us.
The transfigured word is a bell.
Friendship is a star on our forehead.

Notes

The Irrelevant Man is different from *Un ami, un nuage* (Le Noroît, 2013). The title of the latter ("A friend, a cloud") comes from words spoken by Filippo Tommasso Marinetti at the funeral of his dear friend and sculptor, Umberto Boccioni, who died at thirty-three, from complications following injuries he suffered from a horse fall. One is not the translation of the other. Poems get written in various languages. I remember one being written in French first and a second in English and a third in Italian. Every five years I receive a note from my publisher who inquires about a new manuscript. That is the role of a publisher. To push books out of the writers eating and drinking in his backyard. It took me about one year to put this new book together by pasting fragments, texts, essays, scribbles I had been keeping in notebooks for the past decade.

Lucretius: "I've come to unfasten the knots with which religion tied you" (*On Nature,* Book One, 949-950. My translation.)

Page 13: I was asked to participate in a conference on territory, a theme I shun as much as possible. This poem would not have been written without my reading the poetry of Lord Byron and the essay *Stolen Continents* by Ronald Wright. Part 8: Thanks to Lamberto Tassinari for writing *John Florio: The Man Who Was Shakespeare.* Part 24: The last verse is an Arabic proverb. Part 25: The second to last verse is an Italian proverb. Part 26: The last verse is a Corsican proverb.

Page: 37 This poem was written in Halifax, Nova Scotia, after my first visit to Pier 21, where my maternal grandfather, Filippo Salvatore, set foot in November 1913, at seventeen-years-old with twenty-five dollars in his pockets.

Page 41: The lines in Italics are by Robert Bresson.

Page 50: The line in Italics are by Jean Cocteau.

Page 68: This poem has been put to music by Dominic Mancuso.

Page 90. The lines in Italics are by Pier Paolo Pasolini.

Page 107: A scribble produced during a talk on copyright. What was

I thinking of? Is it my translation of an Italian poem? Is it a copy of a known poem? Who am I plagiarizing here? Excuse my digression.

Page 123: The lines in Italics are by Jean-Luc Godard.

Page 125: The Italian alphabet contains 21 letters (the others, *j, k, w, x*, and *y*, are found in borrowed words from other languages).

Page 129: "Allora Gino," written in Italian, was first published in German in Gino Chiellino, *Rem tene verb sequentur: Gelebte inter-kulturalität*, 2011. Thanks sent to Szilvia Lengl, the translator.

A character, the devil, appears throughout this work. Its meaning is specific. Allow me to quote Elaine Pagels from her excellent book, *The Origin of Satan* (Vintage, 1996): "In Hebrew, the angels were often called "Sons of God" *(ben e 'elohim)*, and were envisioned as the hierarchical ranks of a great army, on the staff of a royal court... In Biblical sources the Hebrew term *satan* describes an adversial role. The Greek term *diabolos*, later translated 'devil,' literally means 'one who throws something across one's path'... this greatest and most dangerous enemy did not originate, as one might suspect, as an outsider, an alien, or a stranger. Satan is not the distant enemy but the intimate enemy – one's trusted colleague, close associate, brother" (39, 49).

In my Abruzzese-Molisan dialect, spicy peppers are called "little devils." There are plenty of those around on tables everywhere.

I would like to thank France Mongeau, Viviane Ciampi, Stéphane Despatie, Pierre Bastien, *Exit*, Ghila Sroka, *La Tribune juive*, Danielle Schaub, Louis Royer, Les Éditions du Trait d'union, Franz Benjamin, Jo-Anne Elder, *Ellipse*, Yolande Villemaire, Claude Beausoleil, Carole Rivest, David Goudreault, le spectacle Totempoésie, Francis Catalano, Jean-Éric Riopel, André Roy, Yannick Renaud, *Estuaire*, Claudine Bertrand, Yves Dion, Diego Creimer, *The Apostles Review*, Monica Lavín, *Laberinto* (Mexique), Fulvio Caccia, *Combats* (France), Le Sabord, Alessandra Ferraro, Maura Felice, *Il Tilomeo* (Italie), Jacques Rancourt, Jennifer Dale, Dominic Mancuso, Roger Des Roches, Jean-Marc Desgent, Patrick Lafontaine, Mylène Durand, Pierre-Yves Pépin, Nicola Zavaglia, John O'Meara, Angela D'Alfonso, Jason Trudeau, Tanya

LoBlanco, Paul Bélanger, Michael Mirolla, Connie McParland, Ana Lucía Silva Paranhos, and Elisabeth Pouyfaucon. Each one helped in the writing of this book. Special gratitude is made to my daughter, Elisa Chiocca D'Alfonso and my parents, whose support made it possible for me to think up this work.

By the Same Author

POETRY

La chanson du shaman à Sedna (1973)

Queror (1979)

Black Tongue (1983)

The Other Shore (1985)

L'Autre rivage (1986)

L'amour panique (1987)

Julia (1992)

Panick Love (1992)

L'apostrophe qui me scinde (1998)

Comment ça se passe (2001)

Getting on with Politics (2002)

Antigone (2004)

Bruco (2005)

Un homme de trop (2005)

Un ami, un nuage (2013)

NOVELS

Avril ou l'anti-passion (1990)

Fabrizio's Passion (1995)

La passione de Fabrizio (translated by Antonello Lombardi, 2002)

Un vendredi du mois d'août (2004)

A Friday in August (translated by Jo-Anne Elder, 2005)

L'Aimé (2007)

ANTHOLOGIES

Quêtes: Textes d'auteurs italo-québécois (with Fulvio Caccia, 1984)
Voix off: Dix poètes anglophones du Québec (1985)
Found in Translation: An Anthology of Poets from Quebec (2013)

ESSAYS

In Italics: In Defence of Ethnicity (1996)
Duologue: On Culture and Identity (with Pasquale Verdicchio, 1998)
En italiques: Réflexions sur l'ethnicité (2000)
Gambling with Failure (2005)
Etnilisuse kaitskes (translated by Reet Sool, 2006)
In corsivo italico (translated by Silvana Mangione, 2009)

TRANSLATIONS

The Clarity of Voices, by Philippe Haeck (1985)
The Films of Jacques Tati, by Michel Chion (1997)
Le paysage qui bouge, by Pasquale Verdicchio (2000)
Dreaming Our Space, by Marguerite Andersen (2003)
On Order and Things, by Stefan Psenak (2003)
The Blueness of Light, by Louise Dupré (2005)
The World Forgotten, by Paul Bélanger (2005)
The Last Woman, by Claudine Bertrand (2008)
The Man Who Delivers Clouds, by José Acquelin (2010)
twohundredandfourpoems, by Roger Des Roches (2011)
Un bonheur inattendu, by Marella Caracciolo Chia (2012)
Wings Folded in Cracks, by Jean-Pierre Vallotton (2013)
Beyond the Flames, by Louise Dupré (2014)
Hours, by Fernand Ouellette (2014)
The Body Vagabond, by Martine Audet (2014)

"For more than thirty years, Antonio D'Alfonso has been producing an original and multidimensional oeuvre that includes autobiography, politics, the quotidian, myth, tragedy and humour. Which explains its baroque character... This mixture of geographies is what creates this poet who stands in the middle of people and things and speaks a singular language comprised of bumps and leaps and a syncopated syntax. The comical pesters the dramatic non-stop as if to bend the human condition under the effort of a lived spirituality. In spite of these trials and tribulations, the poet does not forget that to be human means he is a lyrical clown and a dangerous thinker."

Paul Bélanger,
Le Bulletin des Éditions du Noroît, 2013

"The poeticality of Antonio D'Alfonso's texts are often found in the social side of emotional thought. Its appears in the figure of the man of honesty who questions without end his place in the City and the commerce he entertains with his fellow citizens. Politically charged poems, and his poems of introspection bring to the fore a linguistic dimension where the mot juste is incarnated as his identity... as a gesture of love for the people close to him, for the people he spends time with, for the writers he reads. It is the admission of a persistent passion that turns hearts upside down, and is a stubborn quest for significance. Perhaps Antonio D'Alfonso is a philosopher who puts on the mask of the poet in order to better grasp the ambiguities of our world."

Hughes Corriveau, *Le Devoir*, 2013

"What are the excuses that bring a man to count the sentence beats that his body pronounces? He could have, he should have won his bread and butter dancing in some cabaret. At least, there, he would have helped the working man and woman to forget their fatigue. But no, there he is digging into the paper fabric with the hope of hearing, like an ethnologist, the echoes of an ancient consciousness. Out of bounds, *uomo fuori scopo*, this man has produced a lengthy page bearing the title *The Irrelevant Man*. The bustle comes from paper being scratched. The events here revealed are stories, traits, attacks, blows, screams. What he would not do to lift himself from the tiles in the mansions of poetry."

Antonio D'Alfonso

Printed in March 2014
by Gauvin Press,
Gatineau, Québec